Against the Current

Against the Current:
Reflections on the Misuse of Religion

by John Garvey

Templegate Publishers
Springfield, Illinois

First published in 2005 by
Templegate Publishers, LLC
302 East Adams Street
P.O. Box 5152
Springfield, Illinois 62705-5152
217-522-3353
templegate.com

ISBN 0-87243-268-8
Library of Congress Control Number 2005929736

Much of this book first appeared in different form,
in *Commonweal.*

Cover photo by Thomas Elliott Watson

For Maria and Hugh
(and Daniel, and Andrew and Timothy;
and Aimee, and Violet and Desmond)

Contents

Introduction

If there is one thing that can be said to unite religious traditions, it is that most of them begin with the sense that there is something wrong. We know that we are not as we should be, or could be; we know also that something is wrong with the way things are. (This sense might also be what separates human beings from other animals.) We may call this sense the fall, or original sin, or illusion—but the idea that something separates us from the world as it should be, ultimate reality, freedom from illusion, is universally present.

Our popular culture plays around with the same sense, but at an extremely shallow level. Self-help books imply that this sense of separation from whatever it is that is real and true and good can be remedied by following the steps outlined in a few hundred pages. Advertising suggests that your sense of separation can be overcome by buying the product at hand. And many forms of popular religion say that by joining a particular church or movement, or by taking up a particular spiritual practice, the discomfort which seems built into our daily lives as a kind of ever-present white noise will vanish, and we will feel ourselves confidently on the right path. In traditional cultures, at least, the deeper religious and philosophical traditions were honored, and challenged this sort of shallowness. Ours is perhaps the first culture in which what distracts us all—advertising, television, and politics— is all that unites us.

What I want to present here is a counter-vision. I am a Christian, an Orthodox priest, and not at all a relativist where the idea that there is such a thing as truth is concerned. But I believe we really must challenge the idea that a genuine spirituality is something that can be undertaken as if it were a form of therapy, something to make us feel better about ourselves, reconciled to this barbed, difficult, often tragic world. True spirituality will take us into periods of distress and failure. It may help see us through them, but it is always a process, and there is no point at which we can say, "I've arrived." The essays that follow are offered in the hope of defining a spirituality worthy of grown-ups.

There is such a thing as progress in the spiritual life, but it often is not apparent for years, and there are no quick paths. You might get some lucky breaks, but that's all they are. You will need help, and maybe some difficult criticism, to get very far. But help is out there, and progress does happen, and there is such a thing as wisdom. It has almost nothing to do with information, and everything to do with insight.

Chapter 1

Making Use of Religion

There is a mysterious moment in the Acts of the Apostles. A sorcerer named Simon has converted to Christianity. "Now when Simon saw that the Spirit was given through the laying on of the Apostles' hands, he offered them money, saying 'Give me also this power, that anyone on whom I lay my hand may receive the Holy Spirit.' But Peter said to him, 'Your silver perish with you, because you thought you could obtain the gift of God with money! You have neither part nor lot in this matter, for your heart is not right with God. Repent therefore of this wickedness of yours, and pray to the Lord that, if possible, the intent of your heart may be forgiven you...' And Simon answered, 'Pray for me to the Lord, that nothing of what you have said may come upon me.'"

There is something a bit poignant here. Simon was an apparently sincere convert, and his response to Peter is hardly arrogant. His story has been used throughout the ages to illustrate the wrongness of buying or selling church positions and blessings. (The word for such illicit activity is "simony," after Simon.)

The meaning, however, is surely deeper than this. Simon thought that he could make use of religion to enhance his own power. He believed that this enhanced power was something he could attain. At one level, of course, he was wrong to think that the power he sought was something he could buy. But money is only one way to obtain something; it is hardly the only medium of exchange, even if one of the crudest.

Simon was sincere. At the moment when he asked if he could buy the power the apostles exercised, he was unaware that he was doing anything wrong. His problem was that he was still too encased by everything which had formed him—all of the habits of thinking and feeling that made him the man he was. Something in him, something which was the seed of whatever he was meant to become as a Christian, was capable of responding to the apostles' teaching. But there was something else in him, and it was capable—with all the best intentions in the world—of being profoundly misled. That something else, that bundle of formed responses which is a great deal of what we consider ourselves, responded with a profound misunderstanding of what the power of God means.

This story is especially mysterious in a time that makes sincerity a virtue and in which good intentions count for so much. The idea that it is possible to go radically in the wrong direction even if you want, with all your heart, to do the right thing is disturbing to us, and seems profoundly unfair. It is also unfair (to use a line Kurt Vonnegut once used) when a blind grandmother hits a roller skate at the top of a flight of stairs—she certainly didn't mean to do that—but it happens in the universe we live in.

The point of religious traditions is in part to make us aware of the fact that wanting to do the right thing is not quite the same thing as knowing the right way. Good intentions can lead us over cliffs, and a wily approach, if it is headed in the right direction, may serve us better than sincerity. This could be part of the meaning of Jesus' mysterious lines about making friends with the mammon of iniquity. It certainly has something to do with his counsel that we should be "wise as serpents and innocent as doves."

What is distressing about the current American use of religion and spirituality is precisely that it is a use. Much Buddhism in America is, in comparison with Buddhism as it is encountered on the ground in largely Buddhist countries, so cleansed of asceticism and doctrinal force that it couldn't scandalize a Unitarian. There are Sufis who deny that Sufism is really Islamic in any essential way; it is instead the surfacing of an eternal truth which happened to take place in Islam. Some Christian mega-churches downplay doctrine, finding that it turns off the young members they seek to attract. Various forms of spirituality have been advanced as if they could be encountered seriously, without taking seriously the traditions from which they grew. This is especially true of some trendy approaches to the Kaballah.

Chogyam Trungpa, a Tibetan Buddhist who founded the Naropa Center in Boulder, Colorado, wrote an interesting book called *Cutting through Spiritual Materialism.* According to Trungpa, "The problem is that ego can convert anything to its own use, even spirituality. Ego is constantly attempting to acquire and apply the teachings of spirituality for its own benefit….We attempt to find a self-justifying answer for every question. In order to reassure ourselves, we work to fit into our intellectual scheme every aspect of our lives which might be confusing. And our effort is so serious and solemn, so straightforward and sincere, that it is difficult to be suspicious of it."

There is a temptation to strip away from a religious tradition everything that does not clearly speak to the condition of the modern Western world. The problem is that this is not so simple in practice, whether the practice is that of Buddhism moving West, or Christianity in Asia. The Epistles of Paul, the apostolic church, and the church of the early Middle Ages emphasized different, though not contradictory, aspects of our relationship to Christ and to the Church; medieval Christians saw another facet of the truth, as did Christians during the era when slavery began to be seen for the evil it was.

Tradition in its most subtle and strong sense is the harmony in all of these voices. It is not a distillate which any one of us can perceive to be right and true. During the Enlightenment a certain reductionism began to infect the way we look at tradition. Thomas Jefferson, a deist, thought that what mattered in Christianity was Jesus' moral teaching. He published an edited version of the Gospel that left out the miracles and the resurrection.

We cannot assume that our point of view is more privileged than that of someone else in the history of our tradition. We should try to see what in a religious tradition makes it a conciliar thing, formed of many voices, and we should approach the attempt to learn from any tradition with humility.

A tradition can be seen as a fossilized thing, but it should be seen as a language before which the language's sharer must be humble. It does not exist for the hearer and speaker of the language as she is, presently, to use in a way which reinforces her present status or point of view. It is meant instead to transform the hearer and speaker of the language, to bring the hearer into the deepest experience the tradition has to offer.

The Eastern Orthodox belief is that, even granting historical limitations and cultural limitations, the language which over the years has become the language of prayer and worship can be Spirit-bearing when full attention is paid to it. This is easier to say than to live out, because self-deception is part of the human enterprise, and it is too easy to mistake an emotional or self-justifying response to the words of worship for real attention.

The only alternative is humility, an honesty about unknowing. And this is constantly challenged by our need to be right.

The problem with approaching any religious or spiritual teaching, or any sacred text, is that we think we can know what it means pretty clearly, and we are often startled to find out how much it agrees with our own beliefs. Take the way people typically use the Bible: pacifists will point to Jesus telling Peter to put his sword away; militarists can point to Luke 22, where Jesus tells his disciples that his original instructions on traveling light have changed: "But now, let him who has a purse take it, and likewise a bag. And let him who has no sword sell his mantle and buy one."

In *The Everlasting Gospel* William Blake wrote, "The Vision of Christ that thou dost see/Is my

Vision's Greatest Enemy.../Thine loves the same world that mine hates,/Thy Heaven Doors are my Hell Gates."

We are tempted constantly to make use of Christ, or any concept of God. To the extent that we do this, we make an idol of God. It is difficult for us to realize that it is possible for us to worship a false god, believing with all our hearts that it is true. If we firmly believe that our cause is just, if it seems to us that anything that contradicts our vision is immoral or dangerous or contemptible, it seems a natural move to seize upon the authority of the Bible (or of a tradition, or the words of some great teacher) to back us up. But in doing this we overlook the contradictory and equally authoritative passages of scripture or elements of tradition; and we deal with this by saying that our own interpretation is a reflection of the real spirit of scripture or of the tradition. Our opponents—who are apparently farther removed from the Holy Spirit than we are—don't understand this.

No matter how good our intentions are, or how noble the cause, this is a form of idolatry. What concerns us is not God's truth, which is at its depths unknowable and absolutely incomprehensible, but ideas which seem to us to be true. We can be so passionately attached to these ideas that we find it impossible to believe that God does not share our opinion.

Is there any way out of this dilemma? It really is a dilemma and one which matters deeply not only to our way of approaching morality at personal and social levels; it matters to our relationship with God. On the one hand, we cannot be so open-ended about moral and spiritual issues that absolutely anything is considered as true as anything else. On the other, we must avoid the idolatry which makes an idol of our own belief.

The temptation is to look for some clear standard of truth. This happened in the nineteenth century with the rise of three apparently contradictory movements, which are at root very similar. One was scientism, another was Protestant fundamentalism, and the third was Roman Catholic infallibilism. Scientism (found today in such thinkers as Richard Dawkins, Steven Pinker and E.O. Wilson) believes that the only truths that matter can be found only through the use of the scientific method. Fundamentalism sought certainty in a literal reading of scripture, which was seen as totally free of error. With the declaration of the infallibility of the Pope, Catholics were assured that anything concerning faith and morals, said ex cathedra (from the throne) by the Pope, could be known with certainty to be true. What all three of these have in common is the need for certainty, the inability to entertain any "on the other hand" possibilities.

We are not sufficiently humble before the fact that every convinced Nazi, Fascist, Communist, crusader, inquisitor, book-burner, vigilante, or member of a lynch mob had a burning conviction that he was in the right, and stood where he stood against the forces of wrong-headedness or absolute evil. Our conviction, being right, is of course a different thing.

What we need is a truly radical humility, one which can abandon any need to be right. This is terribly difficult, because it could seem to be an indifference to truth. But our need to be right has nothing to do with any love for the truth. It is essential for us to understand this.

Jesus said, "Your eye is the light of your body: when your eye is sound, your whole body is full of light; but when it is not sound, your body is full of darkness. Therefore be careful lest the light in you be darkness" (Luke 11: 34-35). He does not say that it will not appear to us to be light; he cautions us that what seems to be light may in fact not be.

According to Gregory of Nyssa, one of the Fathers of the Church, "concepts create idols; only wonder comprehends anything." People kill one another over idols. Wonder makes us fall to our knees. This is the way to seek the truth: to know that we do not have it—in the sense that we are in possession of it—but that we may participate in it if we approach it humbly, from beneath, knowing we cannot exhaust it.

The tradition to which I belong says that we have been called into being from nothingness, and given a freedom which is not at all easy to comprehend, and can never be comprehended completely. Prayer and meditation are the ways we approach seeing what all of this means because in prayer and meditation—in the effort to be attentive—we learn how radically contingent we are, how absolutely dependent on someone unknowable. That we have been called forth from nothingness, in love, is revealed, not as a fact but as an openness which can be responded to honestly only with an emptiness of our own, an acknowledgement of our own absolute insufficiency. This emptiness is the place where compassion can be born; because it is absolutely shared with everything else in creation, it is the common ground of our being.

"When the eye is sound the whole body is full of light." How can we be sure that the eye is sound? It could be that sureness is not what is called for here, but humility. Jesus tells us not to look for ways to be sure, but rather to take care, to watch. Gregory of Nyssa's words suggest that a lack of the sense of wonder leads to idolatry. Only a lack of wonder could lead us to look at what scripture and tradition tell us, and come up with concepts. This is true not only of theologians but of any believer who imagines that a proper religious life comes down to having the right ideas.

The need to be right fills us up. It leads us to ignore the emptiness that is part of being created.

Chapter 2

Religion, Morality, and the Need to be Right

Blake wrote that if Christianity is morality, then Socrates is the savior. The point is essential, but for many believers—not only politicians aiming at re-election and people who want to prove their morality to their neighbors—the idea that religion is not primarily about morality would be baffling. Your average secular dismisser of religion speaks easily about religion as a means of social control. Your average right-wing Christian tends to agree with this simple-minded nonsense, in practice and even at times in theory: how are you going to keep them down on the farm (and away from the sheep) unless you threaten them with hell, or worse, law?

There is no denying that religion has been used as a form of social control. So has politics; so have power and influence within political systems; so has the denial of tenure in universities. There is a stream of connections between religion and morality, and I don't want to make too little of it. But making too little of it really isn't our problem these days, when many people who are against pornography and nuclear weapons and racism and abortion and the death penalty claim some religious sanction for their point of view. They are right to a very important extent. I am against all of the above; I am also unsure in many cases about what the varieties of law available in the United Sates ought to do about any of this array of problems, and I think, finally, that what we think of as religion and what we think of as morality have relatively little to do with one another.

What worries me here is the capacity we all have for astonishing depths of self-deception. There may be some very rare people who believe themselves to be sincerely duplicitous and hypocritical, but I haven't met them. I don't know many people who believe themselves to be anything other than absolutely right on any point which matters deeply to them. Our attachment to our ideas fills emotional needs which often have nothing to do with the ideas themselves, and we are in danger when we deny this. This is especially true of ideas involving morality, and in our times morality and politics, or morality and law, are frequently intertwined.

It is easy to see why morality, including social morality, matters so much to us. When we speak of the way people should or should not behave, at the personal or the social level, we are speaking of what we think matters most in human life. And where some absolutely conflicting views are concerned, both parties cannot be right—one must be right, and the other wrong, with regard to such important questions as whether abortion is a reasonable and acceptable form of birth control, or whether the state should be allowed to kill criminals. Christianity does address many moral issues, has something to say about them, and we must not ignore this. But there is something infinitely more to Christianity than its moral vision.

It has been pointed out by a number of writers that Christianity sheds light on such subjects but has no specific political agenda; good people may disagree on the best ways to achieve desirable ends. But even those good ends are not Christianity's highest vocation. A world where peace and social justice reign is a desirable human goal, but it is not the point of Christianity.

The Jews whose country the Romans occupied during Jesus' time had an obvious moral grievance, and the world of the Roman Empire was one that included the evil of slavery. But the radical change of heart that Jesus called for had to do with something much more profound than the question of who was right or wrong about slavery or the occupation of Palestine.

One implication of this is that we are concerned with the wrong questions when we worry about who has the power, or who among those who seek power—even for the best reasons—is right or wrong. We are like people in a dream who have to choose between the green shoe and the orange monkey, a choice that makes wonderful sense in a dream and may even have a compelling logic there, but which, in the light of something we cannot now see (because we are now awake), is deluded.

Our justice is not God's. When the gospels speak of a mercy which falls on the just and the unjust alike, they do not refer to a form of justice or righteousness which we instinctively want to share. It is vital that we understand how little even our best instincts and moral passions have to do with God's love for us. Jesus' own apparent indifference to the most important social questions of his age ought to matter to us. It doesn't give any comfort to supporters or opponents of the status quo. The implication is that our questions, our concerns, are wrong. Our major problems have so much to do with our hearts—not ours in some collective sense, but yours, and mine—that political questions can be a luxury and distraction for us. If it were possible to abolish all weapons from the face of the earth, eliminate poverty, abolish all forms of bigotry, educate the ignorant, and end the most crippling illnesses, all of the truly important questions would remain. It would be possible to be unloving in such a world. Despair would still be real, and it would be possible to be damned. The world's deepest questions can't be answered politically.

This is not a call for quietism. We should be willing to take and support political action, as long as it is informed by compassion. I don't think, though, that we should call this involvement a Christian thing, or mistake it for the goal of Christianity. It could be that Christian politics is like Christian nutrition or Christian proctology, a concept which we ought to avoid. We can change our politics and morality, given sufficient will, self discipline, and conviction. The transformation we really need is more radical than that, and it is beyond anything we can accomplish by ourselves. That may be what makes morality and politics so appealing.

* * *

One day I walked towards an elevator and reached it at about the same time as a woman who was holding a child; the child was around one-and-a-half or two years old. I pushed the button and the child looked at me furiously. I realized then that he had planned on pushing the button himself. He turned in his mother's arms and slapped her.

This struck me as a nice illustration of child logic: he wanted to push the button; the stranger did it instead; his mother is in charge of the universe and plainly messed up here; therefore she should be punished.

This isn't too far from adult logic. I saw someone turn on a waitress once, angry because a second before he had spilled shrimp sauce on himself. I have been angry at objects (balky computers, hairbrushes) because they would not respond as I thought they should. None of this is far from that child's reaction, if indeed there is any difference at all. A lot of the way we experience the world is filtered through clouds of irritation, unreasonable expectations, fear, and all sorts of self-centered emotions and reactions which effectively keep us from experiencing what Caussade, in a lovely phrase, called "the sacrament of the present moment."

There has not been enough attention paid to the psychology of spirituality. What we need is something which can be found in the desert fathers, the Philokalia—a classic collection of Orthodox spirituality—and in some Buddhist writing. One Buddhist text, for example, refers to the feelings of aversion we experience when confronted, say, by the decaying corpse of an animal, as a form of anger directed at an object, unreasonable in the most profound sense. Several of the sayings of the desert fathers tell us that it is a greater work to conquer anger than to raise the dead. This applies not only to the forms of anger which are obviously outsized and wrong, like yelling curses at inept drivers, or berating a child, but also to the forms of anger we direct at politicians, or the irritations encountered in the course of a normal workday.

The degree to which anger and resentment inform our inner lives would disturb us, I think, if we could see it clearly. The pleasures of resentment are nursed in some small degree by nearly everyone, and in large degree by many. To feel wronged is bracing, in a sour way, a form of pleasure-pain; and to feel that you are kept from your rightful place by someone else (a parent, when you are an adolescent, or a superior in a corporate or religious or governmental structure), or by an unreasonable circumstance, allows the feeling that the world would be as it should be, if only it weren't for—whatever it may be; the pleasure is the same.

A lot of anger—a lot of the kind I have experienced, anyway—comes from the illusion that our time is literally ours, a thing we have a right to, a personal possession, and anyone whose demands mean that I will not get to use it as I wish will be resented. This is part of what I mean by the psychology of spirituality. An approach to this problem which says, "You shouldn't be irritated at the unexpected phone call, the visitor who dropped by without calling first, the need a friend has for a ride—she too is a child of God, and you should be grateful for the opportunity to serve others"…that sort of moralism never got very far with me because if I took it seriously I would go around thinking I deserved some credit for what, in a better person, would pass for simple decency. It also fails to get at the illusion that lies at the root of the irritation.

This illusion is the infantile one that the universe has been structured around what I see as my needs, and if it hasn't been, it should be. Until this illusion is shattered, even "good" uses of my time—things like putting up with someone who bores me, working voluntarily for a good cause, and so forth—are spiritually pointless. I am likely to think that it is good of me to do these things with "my time."

Morality, insofar as it means the self-conscious pursuit of virtue, could be the greatest enemy of spiritual understanding, short of distraction. To behave in a way which you know is moral—whether this means refraining from theft or adultery, or behaving in a positively "good" way through the performance of a generous or courageous act—can reinforce the ego and protect us from self-awareness. I do not mean that we should not behave morally, only that we should not regard moral behavior as much more important than taking out the garbage. The fact that moral behavior can exist apart from prayer ought to teach us that it has relatively little to do with religion or spirituality.

It is an important social necessity, a form of civility. Jesus says that after we have done everything we ought to do, we are still unprofitable servants. One meaning of this could be that morality, doing the right thing, is at most a by-product of spiritual understanding, not its point.

There is no doubt that we should behave morally, and I do not mean to argue for indifference towards morality. But morality does occupy us too much, perhaps because it involves the things we can take care of ourselves, without having to endure any vision of ourselves as completely inadequate, totally contingent. Where asceticism has been at its worst, where it has been misunderstood, has been where it is identified with moral action. Eastern Orthodox spirituality speaks of "guarding the heart"—that is, paying attention to what goes into the heart and how we respond to it. This should apply to everything we encounter, not just those things we tend to think of as spiritual or ethical.

We have to pay attention to the ways in which doing what at the most obvious level we want to do— our desire—leads us around "like a captive corpse," in the words of Orthodox writer Tito Colliander (*The Way of the Ascetics*). This may show us how the thing we think of as liberating can actually be enslaving. How free are we if we feel we must be free to do something we want to do? Meister Eckhart says that the way to imitate Christ's fasting is this: refrain from what you want to do or are most inclined to do (and of course there is a distinction between the two), and watch yourself carefully. Only asceticism of this sort, a willingness to go against what seems to be the grain, can begin to show us the complex depths of our lives, and can reveal the fact that desire and the fulfillment of desire are not necessarily the same thing as freedom.

The end of a prayerful life, the goal of asceticism, should be a clarity of understanding and activity which is denied us when we are incapable because of distraction and self-involvement and the webs of attachment, of simply being before God in the present moment. Saint Seraphim of Sarov addressed each person who came to him as "my joy." (My response to too many people is, "You again?") Most of us are very far from being able to see others, or to see creation itself, as God sees the universe at the moment of creation, knowing it, rejoicing in it, as good.

Chapter 3

Protecting the Ego

An Orthodox bishop once told me that he receives people into the church only after they have been made part of an Orthodox family's life for a year, allowed by the family to worship and share meals and time with them freely. The reason for this is to allow the potential convert to observe Orthodoxy as it is lived on a daily basis. "But," he said, "I always make sure that the family has been Orthodox for at least five years."

I asked the reason for that limitation. He answered, "By then, they should have lost their convert's enthusiasm."

A Trappist monastery I once visited has a program which allows some guests to participate in the lives of the monks to a greater than usual degree, sharing their work and common worship. Participants must stay for at least five days, however. The monk in charge was asked why someone couldn't stay a shorter length of time and still participate. "They need enough time to begin to be bored," he explained. "Without that, you won't begin to understand monasticism."

I'm not sure five days is enough to get bored with monastic life, but the principle is a sound one. Both of these ideas—waiting for "convert enthusiasm" to die off, and seeing what's there after boredom—may offer a way into understanding what the early monastic writers meant when they wrote of "the fires of apatheia."

Our word "apathy" doesn't begin to convey the right sense of the word. A literal translation—away, or apart, from feeling or emotion—sounds a bit chilly, and so does a possible substitute, "detachment." Perhaps the difficulty with a simple definition lies in the fact that the experience is distant from ordinary consciousness, which many commentators have compared to drunkenness, dreaming, or sleepwalking. Any attempt to still the attention can show how the mind jumps from instant to instant, scattering in every direction. Memories of the past and worries or fantasies about the future pull the attention away from the present. Simply to be, in the presence of God and others, is not simple at all. Stillness is sometimes a gift, but it is also in part a learned thing.

Which brings us back to the examples above. What is wrong with a convert's enthusiasm, or with finding the particulars of the monastic life intriguing? Nothing, of course; nor is there anything wrong with enjoying a piece of music you haven't heard before. But even this good thing is, in some important circumstances, a distraction. The idea of apatheia calls on us to question the ordinary place of the emotions in our life.

Our culture teaches us to identify our emotional life with the deepest parts of the self. We are taught to rely on feeling and emotion as guides, and the jargon of pop psychology reflects this: one should "be in touch with" one's feelings, and not repress them. To deny anger, for example—to refuse to acknowledge its presence in us or the way in which it can determine our behavior—can lead to the worst forms of self-deception. And to see nothing in our feelings, to regard them as essentially unimportant or indifferent, is not Christian. Insofar as they have to do with our humanity, they are good.

They are not, however, guides—not, anyway, as we usually experience them. They can be understood properly only with a certain struggle, an effort at attentiveness which does not come easily to us. I was about to write, "does not come naturally to us"—but one point here is that our true nature is obscured, and must be won. This may be one reading of Jesus' words, "the kingdom of heaven suffers violence, and the violent take it by force" (Matthew 11:12).

There are instructive parallels in other religious traditions, in for example the philosophy of the stoics and in Buddhism. Rather than define apatheia abstractly, it is probably a good idea to look at specific situations, to see what can be negative and limiting about our ordinary approach to feeling, and what is positive about the movement toward apatheia.

If someone insults me at an obvious level (say, by calling me ugly or stupid) or at a less obvious level (by telling me that something I have written is shallow, or by laughing at one of my firmly held opinions), my first reaction is to take offense, to feel anger or at least irritation, and to respond in a way which is a direct and emotional reaction—however well it may be disguised in many instances—to the feeling of having been insulted or humiliated. Perhaps one of the reasons apatheia began to impress me as practically helpful was that a number of incidents in my life made it uncomfortably clear to me that my need to be right had little or nothing to do with any love for the truth. That need had to do, instead, with the shoring up of ego: it could pose easily as a concern for truth.

But if truth were really at stake, my response would never involve anger or irritation or triumph (a feeling which is, I am sure, a variation of anger). For instance, if I am in fact ugly, that is simply the case— there's no reason to be upset about it. If I am not, the person who claims that I am has done so to wound me, in which case I should wonder first how I may have caused such offense as to provoke that response; or I should feel compassion for someone who has the need to wound me. In either case, anger isn't the appropriate response. Similarly, if something I have written is shallow or stupid, it is; if not, it isn't—but why be angry? What gets hurt and makes anger arise is the challenge to an image of myself, an image I feel the need to maintain, one which is never ugly, shallow, or stupid. The need to hold onto that image is the most common form of idolatry, and many of our feelings are tied up in the effort. The image does not need to be obviously foolish; it can also be an image of the self as a humble, responsive and loving person, or a prayerful person, or even a person who is open to correction.

The discipline of guarding the heart means paying attention not only to those things which most obviously involve spirituality, but also matters of daily habit and routine, so that the ordinary movements of attentiveness or inattentiveness, attraction and anger and resentment, can be seen more clearly.

Where this idea can go wrong is not when it is applied too strictly, but rather where it is applied too selectively. There is in some of the stoics and in some Christian ascetical writing too exclusive and negative a concentration on sexual temptation or drunkenness or gluttony—obvious passions, all having to do with the body—and this apparent denial of the goodness of the body has led some people to a rejection of asceticism itself. That is unfortunate because finally it is an affirmative, rather than a negative, approach to life. The goal is for our bodies and feelings to assume the places they were meant to have in undistorted form.

There are a number of prayers in Orthodox prayer books that speak of our passions as deluding influences that make us unhappy. If we react to this language by assuming that the passions in question are the ones preachers typically take aim at—lust is probably the first choice there—they can look merely quirky and old-fashioned. But the passions in question, when they are identified, are often such emotions as sadness, or our obsession with bitter memories. One prayer asks for the dispelling of "the dream of despondency." Another asks for "deliverance from my many cruel memories and deeds."

The goal of apatheia is stillness. Perhaps the best image of what it means is the one offered in the gospels, the image of Jesus with his disciples in the storm-tossed boat. They panicked and were afraid, driven by their feelings. They were affronted by the fact that in the midst of the storm Jesus lay at rest, his head on a pillow. It may not be too much to say that apatheia is, finally, a kind of divine nonchalance.

Chapter 4

Choice, Freedom, and the Mystery of Evil

Some years ago I read the horrifying story of an exec-
utive who got into his private airplane with his wife,
took off, and when they were airborne he shot her in
the head, then killed himself by downing a fifth of
scotch in fifteen minutes. Their bodies were found in
the wreckage. This occurred on a planet where at
exactly the same time people watch their children
starving, the sound of television quiz shows fills the
rooms of old people in nursing homes, a woman gives
birth to her first child, someone is moved to tears by
the glory of Bach, sharks feed, frogs snap at flies, a
couple driving on a remote country road wonder what
it would be like to live the lives of the people in the
farmhouses they pass, parents abuse small children, a
walrus dies with something like wonder on his mind,
a young wife on the telephone to her mother forgets

that the roast has been too long in the oven, and monks send up praise to God. Who knows all this.

What a place. As soon as I read the newspaper account of the murder-suicide, I wondered about that murderous husband. What could take a person to such a moment? That question may be the reason there are more good murder mysteries than there are books about war or hit-men. Killing done for political or business reasons we can understand, much as we might loathe it—but what passion could make us do this? What emotion would take us there? What would it be like to go from here to there? To have your world so fill up with a single passion that it crowds everything else out of your life except stopping another person's whole world—this is, among other things, intriguing. And it is important to understand that the murderer is not unlike you or me. A series of choices and surrenders make that moment possible. People speak of being driven to murder, and no doubt that is what it feels like, an uncontrollable passion, a possession by something alien. Even more common forms of anger can feel like this. But it is really the result of choices made beforehand. It is our freedom that makes murder and suicide possible.

That isn't to say that a person at that moment feels free, is not in fact enslaved, controlled. This is the result, however, of lots of small choices and surrenders.

What it feels like now isn't the point, and what it feels like has nothing to do with our freedom.

When I first read the desert fathers, I wondered why they spent so much time dealing with the question of anger. That shows only how young I was when I read them. It is essential to understand the ways anger, anxiety, depression, fear, and even common forms of impatience are all knotted together at the base. This may not bring you any closer to stillness, or it may, but it will at least let you understand the thicket that lies between you and peace a little more clearly. It is very hard to take the advice (make that a command) "Be not afraid" to heart. It involves a struggle.

The fact that choice has been made a primary moral category in our time has caused a lot of commentary; what has not been noted enough is that choosing in a truly free way sometimes involves an intense struggle, and the clarity it requires is hard-won, and there may be no feeling of clarity or satisfaction in the process.

Where choice is seen as something moral in and of itself we have no help at all. Where a certain sort of life is offered as exemplary and another is offered as a cautionary tale, we at least have some sort of guideline, and there is then at least the implication within a culture that some real world exists beyond the realm of the choices at hand, a landscape within which choice takes place. For this reason it makes good sense—it is even an obligation—to hate what our culture offers our children. We are not helped by the fact that saints and other moral heroes mean less to us now than they did to previous Christian generations. It didn't help, though, that their stories were offered to us in ways which minimized their struggles, not showing us (for example) Jerome's problem with anger, Augustine's problem with patience (it is my opinion that he never had enough interesting problems with lust to make him very helpful in that over-advertised Augustinian realm), or Thérèse's problem with depression and doubt. It is also helpful to know that Jerome and Augustine disliked each other.

They struggled against the passions—against the things that rule and take us over, and take some of us to murder. Clarity can begin to come with some distance from the things that move us, more than from identification with them. This goes against the grain of a lot of pop psychology, which would have us vent our anger, allow us our outrages, ask for honesty in the expression of feeling. Honesty in the identification of feeling is certainly essential. It is important to notice what anger does in some specific place in the center of our chests and watch what happens there.

But that feeling is, putting it mildly, not to be trusted as a guide to behavior. It is also important not to worry too much about it as a presence; and to seek too deeply into the sources of anger can be a form of narcissism, though to avoid looking at all at those sources can be a form of unhealthy and destructive denial.

The point is that the passions—the things that move us—are not to be seen as having an automatic claim to authenticity or emotional authority. They are to be noticed, not denied; we have to see the gravitational field they generate, and see it calmly. They are not evil, but they can lead us into evil places, because we are not free, as it is our vocation to be, as long as we feel any compulsion, any drivenness. This freedom is the reason for asceticism, which is not a denial of the flesh but a struggle for clarity.

It could be argued that all human evil consists precisely in the denial of this freedom, everything from war to murder and suicide. One way of approaching the idea of evil is the recognition that something hates humankind and wants to see it destroyed. Our age, which has seen evil on a massive, genocidal scale, denies the reality of evil—which, as C. S. Lewis pointed out, is the devil's greatest victory. Something—I am willing to call it Satan—wants us not to see that we are made in God's image. It is the deepest sort of horror, a terrifying denial of the deepest reality, when someone made in God's image puts a gun to the head of another person made in God's image.

A fascination with evil, though, is another victory for evil. At the center of Christian faith is the fact that evil has been overcome. At the Paschal liturgy of the Orthodox Church, a baptismal sermon of St. John Chrysostom is read, and it is wonderful:

"By descending into hell, he made hell captive. He embittered it when it tasted of his flesh…It was embittered, for it was abolished. It was embittered, for it was slain. It was embittered, for it was overthrown. It was embittered, for it was fettered in chains. It took a body, and met God face to face. It took earth, and encountered heaven. It took that which was seen, and fell upon the unseen. O death, where is thy sting? O hell, where is thy victory? Christ is risen, and demons are fallen. Christ is risen, and the angels rejoice. Christ is risen, and life reigns."

* * *

How are we to maintain a faith this full of joy, in the face of human suffering? Newspapers are full of horrors: we read about children murdered by their mother's boyfriends, or see the misery of mentally ill people who find getting through the day a terrifying prospect—God's presence must be there, and nothing seems to happen for them. Nothing happens for the homeless who freeze to death. God is present in some way in any number of horrible places, and nothing seems to happen.

It's a little like the old tale of stone soup: a hungry soldier promises to show a selfish old lady how to make soup with nothing more than water and a stone, but persuades her it would taste a little better if he could only add a potato, some onions, some meat, some barley—all of which she adds, pleased at how clever she is to learn the secret of making soup with nothing but a stone. Belief in God must look something like this to non-believers, something added and unnecessary, self-deceptive. Marx said not only that religion was the opium of the people, but also called it "the sigh of the oppressed, the heart of a heartless world." What does God's silence in horrible moments tell us about reality, or about God?

This is the old problem of theodicy—the attempt to make sense of the distance that seems to lie between the idea of a good God and a world in which the innocent suffer. In *The Brothers Karamazov,* Ivan Karamazov tells his brother Alyosha stories of children who have been horribly tormented and says, "The whole world of knowledge is not worth the tears of that little child to 'dear God'...I do not, finally, want the mother to embrace the tormentor who let his dogs tear her sons to pieces! She dare not forgive him! Let her forgive him for herself, if she wants to, let her forgive the tormentor her immeasurable maternal suffering; but she has no right to forgive the suffering of her child who was torn to pieces, she dare not forgive the tormentor, even if the child himself were to forgive him! And if that is so, where is the harmony? Is there in the whole world a being who could and would have the right to forgive? I don't want harmony, for the love of mankind. I don't want it. I want to remain with unrequited suffering. I'd rather remain with my unrequited suffering and my unquenched indignation, even if I am wrong. Besides, they have put too high a price on harmony; we can't afford to pay so much for admission. And therefore I hasten to return my ticket. It's not that I don't accept God, Alyosha, I just most respectfully return him the ticket." (*The Brothers Karamazov,* North Point Press, translation by Richard Pevear and Larissa Volokhonsky)

Any believer who has never felt this way lacks a human heart. It is a grace to feel the horror of our true condition, and that is the accuracy of Ivan's reaction; but there is also the desire to control and contain our horror, to make sense of it, and this is where we are helpless, and miss the point. (There is another way, of course, to deal with evil, and that is to abandon any sense that life has a meaning of the sort that makes our

48

suffering seem so terrible, so unjust; from this point of view the tears of the tormented child are only a kind of humidity. This is a philosophically tenable point of view, but most of its adherents don't, thank God, live its consequences out in their personal lives.)

If Christian revelation is essential to what we need to know, then the universe, as we need to understand it, is something we cannot know from within, on its own terms. Christians argue that revelation, the revelation that has made itself known in Christianity, is essential for understanding the universe and God's relationship to it. Anger at God for evil assumes that God is responsible for evil because God is responsible for the universe. This is Ivan's complaint. But in approaching the idea of God and God's responsibility for evil, he assumes, as many have since the Enlightenment, that the God of the deists and the God of Aristotle is the God Christians worship—that is, God as prime mover, God as the uncaused cause, the one who established a set of rules and observes from afar.

A more traditional answer to the problem of evil—still probably the best we will get, if not very satisfying—says that what has made evil possible is not God, but the freedom we have been given. To be made in God's image means that we are created free; to be free is to have the possibility of rejecting even the source of our creation and freedom—that is, to be free to sin. Paul says in Romans 5:12 that death entered the world through sin, and even physical evils—floods, famines, cancer—have been seen by many Christians as the result of sin itself. This is not to say that they are punishments, but signs and consequences of a world in which evil has real power. From one point of view this seems naïve because we assume a universe in which "natural laws" and "evils" have a certain autonomy. We sense a difference between floods or famines or cancers that kill people, which can be accepted with a certain stoicism, and the evils that result from human hatred and human delight in murder and torture—these, because we are more directly responsible, haunt and anger us more.

There seems to be a connection between the two in the Bible. When a man who is schizophrenic murders his neighbor, something connects natural and human evils. Something that arguably has a chemical and involuntary basis moves from the world of natural laws into the world of human agency. Jesus cured people possessed by demons, who did what they did without choice, driven to self-destructiveness as drowning people are killed by floods; he also forgave adulterers, healed the blind, and calmed storms. In the earliest Christian picture of the world, there was no clear distinction between human and natural evil.

Many Christians have accepted a more or less deistic picture of God. We have moved away from

Paul's idea that death and other evils have entered the world because of sin, which is to say because of us, rather than because of God. When we absolve ourselves of our own enormous responsibility for evil, by blaming God for the obviously enormous evil with which we are surrounded, we ignore some clues— some indications at a lower level of what might be causes for evil on high.

Children who come from abusive families often tend to become abusive. A child who has not known love or compassion will have a hard time learning to be compassionate. The only freedom such a child might experience might be the feeling of some remorse at the moment he commits abuse or an act of violence. There is a clue here to how our own indifference to those who suffer can increase evil.

At the same time, there is evidence from the lives of saints that people in families and communities can influence one another in powerfully good ways. St. Basil the Great came from a family full of saints. During World War II a community of French Protestants banded together to save Jews from the death camps. There is something about this that challenges the two-tiered universe of the post-Enlightenment era, in which the natural and supernatural are clearly demarcated. Abusive families have their terrible gravity; but families and communities in which genuine goodness can be found have a similar, powerfully liberating force.

Ivan Karamazov was a young man, bitter, and saw his bitterness as a moral thing. An older man (unlike Ivan, he really existed) was recently canonized a saint of the Orthodox Church: Father Silouan (1866-1938), a monk of Mount Athos, aware of every evil Ivan could imagine, lived constantly with what he claimed was a God-given command: "Keep your mind in hell, and do not despair." This refusal to despair is possible because he believed, unlike Ivan, that there is "in the world a being who could and who would have the right to forgive."

Precisely because of prayer, the reasoning of a saint and the reasoning of someone who is not prayerful at all will work along radically different lines. Reason is not autonomous, and grace does pervade the world. Of course, this can't be proven to anyone, and that in itself is an essential part of what our freedom means.

Chapter 5

Faith and Feeling

There can be an overemphasis on feeling and emotion in religion; but on the other hand, there can be too little. It is not wrong to expect to have some experience of what it means to have faith, to love God, to be loved by God; and just as our experience of a relationship with someone else can and will change over the years, a relationship with God, if it is alive, changes. When religion is reduced to an acknowledgement of a certain set of facts, it is as dead as a marriage that is merely a contractual arrangement. Some marriages do exist that way, but they are not in any profound sense really marriages. They are certainly not what marriages are meant to be.

A word as rich as "love" can and ought to mean a number of things. Love means the desire to be with the beloved; a willingness, one that transcends desire, to accept or bring about what is best for the beloved, even where it conflicts with our own desires or interests; a willingness to accept the otherness of the beloved; an emotion of great warmth at the thought of the beloved; a steady attentiveness...the word can mean any or all of these things. And feelings are often involved in what we mean by love because few of us, thinking of those to whom we are bound by whatever it is we mean by love—thinking, for example, of a lover or mate or children—feel no emotion at all.

The love of God—both God's love for us and our love for God—is in some ways the same and in other ways radically different from what we usually mean by the word. If a word's ambivalence can sometimes serve us, in this case it can also be profoundly misleading.

Some part of what we think of as love involves fear, fear for the beloved, and fear that the beloved will be taken from us; it can lead us to grasp. The love we have honestly for God would not be like this because this relationship, one in which the beloved may be taken from us or leave us, is not true of God. The love we have for God can feel different from other loves because of this. It may not feel as intense as the love which includes fear for the beloved and the fear of losing the beloved, and we may confuse this lack of anxiety with a coolness toward God.

There is something in us that wants to experience the love of God the way we experience the love of someone dear to us, a spouse or child or friend, but some of what we feel about those loves has to do with their fragility and impermanence. The Bible tells us that "love is stronger than death," but much of the ferocity of love has precisely to do with the fear that the beloved may be lost. This is why Orpheus pursues Eurydice into the realm of death.

Isn't it true, though, that "perfect love casts out fear"? Maybe. I wouldn't know, personally, because I can't think of one of my children suffering without fear for that child. Of course my love for my children, for anyone, is far from perfect. But I think of Jesus weeping at the death of Lazarus, or at Gethsemane, where we are told that he felt "greatly distressed and troubled." I think of a friend, whose wife's suffering is a source of suffering for him as well, and perhaps sometimes a source of fear. Though the metaphors we have for God and our relationship to God are only a beginning, they point us in the right direction. Certainly the fact that we call God our father has to do not only with our dependence on God, our source in God, but also with the helpless love parents have for their children: God cannot not love us.

The ambivalence of the phrase "the love of God," which can mean God's love for us or our love for God, reminds me of Meister Eckhart's statement: "The eye with which I see God is the eye with which God sees me." The love of God is transforming—both our love, and God's. We are transformed by loving someone we cannot imagine, by trusting someone we cannot comprehend, by following the clues that point toward a universe created in love, and making the decision that those clues mean more than the clues that point to a meaningless universe, or a universe in which meaning is something humans find, and nothing more, a universe where, in the beginning, there was no word.

God's love, we trust, transforms us as well. Our willingness to trust, to love in the dark after reason and caution give up, is answered by God. It is this answering that makes our love possible. The answer is given before our question. It precedes our love—the Word is there, in the beginning—and gives it birth and form.

The tragedy is that our response, which is something different from our feelings about God or our relationship to God, is so cold and half-hearted. But perhaps this is because unlike our usual loves, for wives and husbands, children and friends, this love is not obviously reciprocated…or the reciprocation is so primary and all-enveloping that we cannot see it. Our lack of a whole-hearted response is a way of hedging our bets; thus we live in an attenuated relationship with God—from our side. For us, faith comes down to a hope, sometimes a thin one, that these things are true, and that we will ultimately know this to be the case. Faith includes that hope, no doubt, but the faith that

Jesus speaks about, the faith that moves mountains, is clearly something more than this.

I once met someone who, I believe, had that kind of faith. The contrast between that faith and my own was like the difference between a fire and the blue bead at the end of a wick just before the flame dies. It was an encouraging experience: until that meeting I was not aware that this kind of faith is a real human possibility.

The fact that the ways we talk about the God revealed to us in Christ and by Christ—as Father, as bridegroom, as husband of the church—reflect aspects of our own experience as parents and husbands and wives can show how limited metaphors can be, even when they point us in the right direction. But they can also reveal how shallowly we know our own experience, which is meant to be transformed and deepened as we grow in faith.

Jesus asks, "When the Son of Man returns, will he find faith on earth?" Our ordinary loves are an important part of this. Any compassion at all, no matter how murky, reflects and participates in the love of God. It is important, however, for us to know that this love, even at its most intensely felt, is only the beginning of our potential for responding, and we are meant to be much more than we allow ourselves to imagine.

Chapter 6

Knowing and Doubt

There is a kind of Christian who challenges you with the question, "Have you met Jesus?" or, "Do you know Jesus?" It's an embarrassing question, and should be, since the answer for most of us, when the question is put this way, would have to be "No." We have met ideas about Jesus, or stories about Jesus, and some of us claim that in the sacraments we encounter the living reality of Jesus (though it is far from clear what we really mean by that), and we pray with the confidence that we are heard. But do we know Jesus, or have a true experience of his presence?

The question, so stated, demands a clear answer: I do know him—or I don't. I've met him—or I have little idea of what that might mean. Something makes us ashamed of a less than straightforward answer and puts us at a disadvantage before the people who seem to be much more clear about all this than we honestly feel we can be. They act as if they were quite clear, quite unambiguously certain about their connection to Jesus.

One response could be to wave away the question entirely, which would be a mistake. The New Testament makes it clear that we are meant to encounter the living Christ. The New Testament itself can be as embarrassing for us to encounter as the fundamentalist's probing question, but not necessarily because there is a direct continuity between them.

For most of us, if we were honest, the answer would be an ambiguous one: I do not not know Jesus. I have some connection with Jesus, however much it may exist on the level of yearning or hope. *A Journey in Ladakh* (Houghton Mifflin, 1983) is an interesting account of a young Englishman's journey to a place in India not far from the Tibetan border, where Tibetan Buddhism is lived and taught. The author, Lawrence Harvey, listens to an Indian businessman's description of the importance of being freed from false perceptions of the self. Harvey asks him, "Have you felt what you are talking about?"

The answer is one that people on many spiritual paths could give: "In moments. Enough to know that it is not nonsense. Not enough to live in constant awareness of its truth." Here there is a spirit close to that of the anguished father, praying for his child's healing: "Lord, I believe; help my unbelief." This also has something in common with Leon Bloy's famous statement: The one sadness is that we are not saints.

It is important to know, however, that this ambivalence is not in itself a bad thing, something to be rejected. Every element of spiritual understanding is important and valuable, including doubt and ambivalence. Torquemada might have been thoroughly, sincerely convinced of his rightness. There is an argument to be made for the case that fanaticism and false clarity are, at their depths, ways of masking doubt, and for many they may be. It is not only possible, however, but highly probable that many fanatics are unambiguously convinced that they are defenders of a truth which is, for them, quite unalloyed with doubt, and they are convinced that an orderly universe demands stamping out those who have not seen the light and who will not be converted. We saw evidence of this on September 11, 2001.

It is an essential Christian teaching that the truth can be known. But there can be a counterfeit truth, and a counterfeit knowing. The person in the hold of the counterfeit cannot, obviously, tell the difference.

This may seem obvious, but needs to be said because of the prevailing distrust of any certainty at all, any conviction that one's beliefs are grounded in a reality which really can be known and experienced. I am prepared to believe that some saints and mystics have encountered God in a way I know I have not. But it is important not to counterfeit that certainty without their struggle, and the struggle will certainly involve the uncomfortable experience of ambiguity, uncertainty, and doubt. The counterfeit can be attained, even after a counterfeit of struggle. The only way to avoid this trap is an acceptance of what cannot be known, a willingness to accept doubt as part of our movement towards God.

There is a tendency to rest at this point, to get to a point of comfort even with unknowing and doubt, and the culture reinforces it. However, there is the fact that we are called to a more intimate experience of the truth. The Indian businessman who speaks of having enough experience to know that "it is not nonsense" still struggles to live "in constant awareness" of the truth. To be comfortable with the position of unknowing and doubt is irreverent, a refusal to go deeper—a little as if the oyster wore its grit as an ornament and not the beginning of a pearl.

This deepening must be honest and unhurried, which means that it will contain a lot of uncertainty and doubt, and new doubts will surface along the way. We have example of the unknowing that Jesus encountered at Gethsemane, when he begged that the trial might pass (as if there were some uncertainty as to whether his suffering and death on the cross was inevitable), and when he said of the end of the world that no one, "not even the Son," knows when it will occur. But there are other doubts as well, doubts that we are more likely to experience: doubts that God is real, for example, or that the universe has any inherent meaning at all; and these may be coupled with the suspicion that our belief is a false consolation, a way of avoiding the hard facts of life. To avoid those doubts or suppress them is to make them disproportionately powerful; and to be defensive about belief in the face of the most profound questions is never to grow into a belief worthy of encountering those questions.

One of the greatest strengths of Dostoevski's *The Brothers Karamazov* is that it deals with the most serious religious questions in an honorable way. Ivan Karamazov's objections to Christianity, offered in the chapter entitled "Rebellion," are among the best possible arguments for a moral rejection of Christianity. They are not answered by his brother Alyosha in a point-by-point way. Instead, we are shown other things: the life of Father Zosima, the generosity of Alyosha's spirit, the power of compassion and repentance and forgiveness. These are in fact the only real answers or clues we get when we are faced with doubt.

There was a Christian community for a couple of generations before there was a New Testament. The spirit moved that community to discern which of the writings floating around the community should be included, and which should not; which letters and gospels were adequate expressions of the mystery of Christ; and which ones might mislead us. That spirit is at work among us now and gives us, if we are attentive and patient, a spirit of discernment that can look for signs of Christ's continuing presence among us.

What is wonderful in the work of such important Christian writers as Dostoevski (or Shusaku Endo, in *Silence*) is that we can see there that "knowing Jesus" means being able to see the continuing life of Christ among us where it is manifested—in compassion, in suffering, in forgiveness and forbearance. Apart from our encounters with God in prayer and sacrament, encounters which often confront us more with a sense of our own emptiness than the feeling of Christ's living presence—and this sense of our own thorough inadequacy is itself a kind of mercy, a revelation—these are the places where we truly can say we know Jesus, and not in argument, or even in the most deeply felt conviction.

Chapter 7

Freedom and Obedience

St. Paul speaks of "the glorious liberty of the children of God," and the freedom of the Christian is a central theme in much Christian writing, early and late. It is easy to see how this would seem to dovetail into some strains of political theology, and to find an echo in the stress, in democratic societies, on freedom. Freedom has been equated with the right to do what you choose, unconstrained by any external coercion. We think of ourselves as most free when we are able to choose between alternatives; and freedom is guaranteed politically when barriers to choice are removed. This has been a major part of the argument in favor of an unrestricted access to abortion, of course, but this is only the most prominent example. There are others—they range form the right to choose suicide to the obviously less controversial right to choose the person you will, or will not marry. In any case, freedom and choice are seen as indivisible.

The idea of obedience is placed in opposition to freedom in most of our minds. The two aren't often compared, but somehow obedience and freedom feel opposed: if you must be obedient, how can you be free at the same time? Obedience is a bothersome concept for us because it brings to mind hierarchy, something that also makes us uncomfortable. The implication is that someone or something above us has a proper claim on us, one which may get in the way of an unrestricted freedom to choose between alternatives. The idea of freedom as it has developed in our kind of democracy is very different from whatever Christian freedom might mean. This is not to say that it is wrong, and I know of no one who would choose to live under a social system which denied us the political freedoms we are used to. But Christian freedom is based in the belief that Jesus is the image of what a truly free human being would be like. For this reason, it is necessary for us to see that obedience has much to do with whatever Christian freedom means.

Of course, the idea of freedom in obedience is open to great abuse. Institutions can insist that they mediate God's will, and some claim that giving them obedience is equivalent to obedience to the will of God. Obedience in the common monastic sense of the word can liberate you from the need to make unimportant decisions, freeing you for other things; it can also work as an evil medium of control in totalitarian societies, some of which are religious. Still, the fact is that freedom in the Christian sense is essentially related to obedience—but this does not mean an obedience to law, or to institutional structures. (Obedience may involve these things—they may help us to be obedient to God—but they are not finally the point.)

What is Christian freedom like, and how it is not like freedom as our culture tends to define it?

St. Maximus the Confessor, involved in a seventh-century controversy over how Jesus could be said to have a human will, referred to the deliberative will—the will that feels compelled to make choices—as a product of sin, a result of the fall. It may be hard for us to understand how the element in us which seems most free—the ability to make choices between alternatives—could be seen as a maimed and crippled thing, not will in its clearest, most liberated state. That understanding is essential in a time when the word "freedom" (like the word "love") has become sentimental and corrupt.

Some of those Christians who helped Jews hide from the Nazis during World War II said that, confronted with the situation, they felt that they had no choice. Were they less free than someone who, similarly confronted, might feel an ability to weigh alternatives and then decide to help (or not to)? In Matthew 25, those who are told that they are inheritors of the kingdom because they fed and clothed and visited the Son of Man when he was in need are baffled: "When did we do this?" They are told that they did it whenever they acted compassionately towards "the least of these my brothers." It is important that they did not know; if they had not been impelled to compassionate action, but had decided to do it because they would then be doing something nice for the Lord, they would (to quote another part of scripture) already have received their reward.

Is a decision to feed the hungry more free than an unreflected-upon action to feed the hungry? Does the experience of choice here reveal true freedom, or some degree of insensitivity and hard-heartedness? Of course making a decision to feed the hungry is better than not feeding them, but it is not necessarily an illustration of us at our best or our most free. It is an illustration of our fallenness that in this situation we can feel a choice, a hesitance, and this is what Maximus meant: there are times when this deliberative, fallen willing is all we can manage. But it is not what we are meant for.

Another decision: once married, I am not free to choose among women other than my wife. Am I less free as a result? Or does the commitment to marriage offer a new freedom, which choice can't comprehend? My love for my children is in some profound sense helpless. I can't decide whether or not to love them, and I would not be more free if I experienced this as a choice. But in my experience these relationships—marriage, fatherhood—have been liberating in a way I could not have imagined before entering them.

A final example is the way in which a painter or poet is led to certain words and word combinations, or colors and shapes. There may be some hesitation and deliberation involved in the process of arrival, but they come from moving towards what is experienced as the one right place, the word or color that needs to be there. A state of real clarity would eliminate hesitation in love, or in language (which may be why Jesus, unique among people quoted in the Bible, began his sentences with "Amen, amen"—meaning, "This is the way it is").

The New Testament Greek word for sin literally means "missing the mark," the implication being that there is a standard against which we are measured and from which we have fallen. Obedience is simply a matter of conforming ourselves to that original, whatever it takes. According to Philippians 2:5-11, it means a self-emptying that has little to do with choice, but rather with vocation: what are we meant to be? Being is the only freedom that matters, in Christian terms. The model we are offered was "obedient unto death." Reduced to the idea of obedience to an institution, this can be blasphemy. However, the alternative definition offered by democratic political structures, the identification of freedom with choice, isn't very helpful. We do have the freedom to reject what we are called to be—that is part of our liberty: God will not coerce us. But the result of taking that choice would not be freedom.

Chapter 8

What Are Miracles For?

There is a common assumption among modern, secular people that in ancient times people were more credulous than they are now—hence the belief in miracles. We know better than to believe in them today. Ancients could believe in a virgin birth, for example, because they knew less than we know today about what is possible or likely.

But this view of the ancient understanding is plainly nonsense. The virgin birth, the raising of Lazarus, and the healing of the blind man were considered worthy of notice precisely because they seemed just as impossible to our ancestors as they do to us.

We shy away from the notion of the miraculous because it shakes up our sense of a predictable world; it challenges the belief that the realm of faith is subjective, private, and essentially sentimental. We are right to try to understand the multivalent meanings in miracle stories, the symbolic importance of the doctrine of the virgin birth, the fact that the forgiveness of sins which accompanies many of Jesus' healings is truly the greater miracle. But we tend to slide into an easy sense that these stories are "merely symbolic," with an accent on the "merely," and symbols reduced to the level of the metaphorical.

On the other side are those believers who regard the miraculous as a kind of proof. A miracle proves nothing. Any phenomenon can be dismissed, or explained in some other way. And alleged miracles can be faked. The annual liquefaction of the blood of Saint Januarius in Naples can be duplicated scientifically, and there is nothing wrong with being skeptical about the motives of churchmen, especially where anything financial is concerned.

Here is the paradox: if you truly have faith in God, you do not need a miracle as proof of anything. If you do not have faith, no seemingly miraculous event will persuade you that faith makes sense. Anything that seems miraculous might conceivably have another, entirely materialistic explanation. But there is a converse to this: seemingly explicable things, apparently mundane moments, may be seen to have a miraculous depth.

In the Orthodox icon of the Transfiguration, the figure of Christ is surrounded by a mandorla, an almond-shaped form which signifies, among other things, something that is visible to the eyes of faith. It occurs to me that an agnostic present at that moment might have been unable to see what was before him or would have explained the light away.

The conviction that miracles can never happen will make us impervious to them. I know of a case where a child who was dying of a brain tumor was cured after his parents had asked a priest to anoint him for healing. X-rays showed no sign that anything had ever been wrong. The child's doctor, an atheist, was no doubt convinced that this was one of those one-in-a-million odd cases where something just goes away. I believe it was a miracle; but I have some sympathy for the doctor. What about all of those people who pray desperately that their children will be healed, whose children nevertheless die? What are miracles for if they happen so randomly and if they are, some might say with understandable bitterness, so unfairly distributed? One child healed in France; thousands of children hacked to death with machetes in Rwanda.

We should understand that miracles are not meant as fixes. Everyone Christ healed eventually died of something else. Lazarus, raised from the dead, died later. What are miracles for?

We think of the miraculous as something that intervenes with nature from outside, suspending nature's laws. The alternative to this is a sacramental view of nature. Philip Sherrard, in *The Eclipse of Man and Nature* (Inner Traditions/Lindisfarne Press,

1987), says that "nature is not something upon which God has acted from without. It is regarded as something through which God expresses himself from within. Nature, or creation (the terms are interchangeable in this context), is perceived as the self-expression of the divine, and the divine is totally present within it….Like the Eucharist, nature is a revelation not merely of the truth about God but of God himself. The created world is God's sacrament of himself to himself in his creatures: it is the means whereby he is what he is. Were there no creation, then God would be other than he is; and if creation were not sacramental, then God would not be its creator and there would be no question of a sacrament anywhere. If God is not present in a grain of sand, then he is not present in heaven either."

A friend sent me an essay which contained a wonderful quote from the French poet Paul Eluard: "There is another world, and it is in this one." Our ordinary perceptions are flat and two-dimensional. Something must take us deeper if we are to understand and live as fully as we sense we can. The miraculous is one way in which this deepening happens: we are pointed to the real, to a world in which we are meant not to suffer and die, but to live fully. Miracles fix nothing, but point forward to the age to come, the time when "death shall be no more, neither shall there be mourning nor crying nor pain…"

The Bible is full of anticipated things. The bread and wine broken at the Last Supper point towards a crucifixion yet to occur, and towards the Eucharist in which we celebrate Christ's continued presence among us. The Transfiguration points forward to a Resurrection which had not happened yet. The miracles of healing point to a world to come. The Kingdom that lies ahead but also, as the Eluard quote can remind us, within, is a Kingdom which is implicit now, and is revealed not only in the miracles that astonish us, but the daily miracles (forgiveness, the experience of great beauty, selfless love) that do not astonish us enough.

Chapter 9

Living As If It Were True

Doubt and faith go together. This is said often and too easily. It is true, in its way, but we console ourselves with this line and keep ourselves from being really challenged by genuine faith, or genuine doubt.

Doubt isn't a single or simple thing. From one point of view it is an intellectual discomfort, a sort of cramp in reasoning, a mental speed-bump. It is the necessary part of us that forever sings, "It ain't necessarily so." Isn't there another way to look at this? At the level of reasoning clearly about anything, deliberate and even systematic doubt is essential.

But doubt is also an emotional response. Trust too much and you might be disappointed. Better to hedge your bets, as in Pascal's wager. Pascal's wager, you will recall, says that you can approach the idea of faith this way: if you refuse to accept Christianity, assuming it to be false, and live as your desires dictate, then you lose eternity if Christianity is true. If you accept

Christianity and live as a Christian should, you will have given up comparatively little, but if Christianity is true you will have gained eternal life. As a bet, it makes much more sense to accept Christianity.

At one level this makes some intellectual sense, but I am not sure that what it encourages is anything like faith, at least not the faith that Jesus talks about in the gospels, though it might increase church attendance.

But aren't we all in some way living out Pascal's wager? Here I am not denying that doubt accompanies faith. However, if faith is the substance of things hoped for, we are ordinarily much too weak in our hoping. Paul speaks in Romans of Abraham "hoping against hope," and this is the sort of hope and doubt that Christians all know at crucial moments. Faith is not simply certitude—that would remove the freedom we must have. Faith is a surrender and submission, not the response to something proven, like a problem in algebra. But hoping against hope implies a determined hoping. This is what we lack.

If I really hoped for, yearned for, the coming of Christ—if I truly believed that the good news of reconciliation is true—would I live the way I do? We live ethically, in a crude way, refraining from adultery and murder and intentional rudeness, as well we should. But much of our morality is a refraining from, a not doing, with an occasional decent deed, the coin in the beggar's cup. It is not, ordinarily, living in response to the depth of love shown in the crucifixion, in the hope (and the fearlessness that should accompany the hope) that the resurrection is a grounded hope.

Real faith can't hedge bets. It means taking the chance that it is all meaningless and still stepping off into the dark, living as if the hope is grounded. You can't intellectually or emotionally know that you won't be wrong. But you can hope that on the last day it will be revealed that you were not, and you can risk living that way.

St. Thérèse of Lisieux experienced profound darkness during the last eighteen months of her life. She wrote, "I get tired of the darkness all around me, and I try to refresh my jaded spirits with the thoughts of that bright country where my hopes lie; and what happens? It is worse torment than ever; the darkness itself seems to borrow, from the sinners who live in it, the gift of speech. I hear its mocking accents: 'It's all a dream, this talk of a heavenly country, bathed in light, scented with delicious perfumes, and of a God who made it all, who is to be your possession in eternity! You really believe, do you, that the mist which hangs about you will clear away later on? All right, all right, go on longing for death! But death will make nonsense of your hopes; it will only mean a night darker than ever, the night of mere nonexistence."

(Quoted in *Heaven in Ordinarie* by Noel Dermot O'Donoghue, Templegate, 1979)

At the end, Thérèse found peace and joy, but not without the cost of the terrible burden she described in her autobiography, the enduring of serious doubt, doubt not as an intellectual exercise but as the consequence of serious hope. It may well be that Thérèse was a victim of depression, but in a sense this is beside the point, because genuine doubt of the sort that accompanies every believer is a consequence of serious hope, and does not need to be courted—it will be there. Here is Abraham's hope against hope.

Think of what we claim to believe. We believe that a God who created an immense universe from nothing loves us to the point of being willing to suffer for us, that death is not what we are called to, that we are meant to rise from death as the incarnate God did. To live as if this were true, to hope deeply that it is so, will lead us to doubt, and the more total and intense our hope, the more powerful our doubts will be. We look for the kingdom to come, but the agnostic in all of us suggests that this desire for completeness could be a neuronic trick. The desire for completeness is not proof that the completeness exists, but could be an evolutionary carrot and stick…

There is no proof. There are clues, which seem to point in both directions, but no proof. So faith is not a question simply of adding up the possibilities and risks and taking the least risky way. As Thérèse's example makes clear, there is a great emotional risk in believing and in acting as if the belief were true, and (contra Pascal's wager) belief is not the lesser risk, if it is lived. Although it is true that many saints have spoken of an assurance and confidence that come with faith, when these things come they come as gifts—it isn't guaranteed that we will not face Thérèse's darkness.

Living as if what we what we say we believe were true would mean living with a fearlessness which we usually lack. We live as if death will cancel us completely, in the sense that our fear of death drives us in many directions: to shore up our egos, to hoard against disease and starvation, to wall off those who remind us of our limitations and mortality—the old, the mad, and the ill. The greater risk is not to live this way, but to live as if we are called to rise from the dead, hoping that on the last day it will be revealed that we were not crazy.

Chapter 10

Finding Truth in Beauty

One of the most frightening images from the last century is that of the not uncommon sort of concentration camp guard who could move from a day filled with the business of humiliating, tormenting, and murdering other human beings, to his home, where he could put his children to bed with great tenderness, and listen to Mozart, weeping at the beauty of the experience.

The connection between perception, sensing, sensibility—the realm of the aesthetic—and the kind of knowledge we can articulate and act upon is not at all clear. But it is essential that we try to understand the connection as deeply as we can. One of the great myths of the Enlightenment is that education, an acquaintance with art and literature and the great thought of the past, can make us better people and moral members of society. World War II should have ended the power of that myth, but it lives on despite all the evidence.

It is easy to see why it is so seductive, and especially seductive to people who have experienced the great power of art to bring us into the presence of beauty, sometimes so forcefully that it literally takes your breath away. When I read the first of Rilke's *Duino Elegies*, when I came to the last paragraph of Joyce's *The Dead*, I felt great stillness and astonishment. I felt that I had been changed in some way, and if I didn't betray the moment, things would not be the same for me from now on.

This experience is, to be sure, as fuzzy at one end as it is intense at the other. How would things not be the same? What would it mean, not to betray that stillness—only that I should remember it? That might be enough; but simply to have been brought to the edge of a mystery seems to be enough, at the aesthetic level, and not nearly enough, at the level of action.

The purpose of art is not to make us better people, nor is art a form of moral exhortation. It is in fact possible for great art to participate in great evil, for art to be aesthetically impressive and to degrade, at the same time. (For example, there is a genuine sadism in some of Picasso's portraits of weeping women.) But that isn't what interests me about the question of the relationship between art and the spirit. What I am interested in is the ability of the Nazi to read Rilke or listen to Bach and continue to be a Nazi with no apparent internal contradiction. I cannot say he is not moved to the same stillness I am. But what do we think we have found there, either of us?

This is related to another problem: the behavior of many of the artists and writers who can move us this way. Dostoevski was capable at once of writing *The Brothers Karamazov* and of behaving quite boorishly; Tolstoy was often as full of delusion and self-pity as he was capable of brilliant insight. Walker Percy once said that the only two writers he could think of who were also decent human beings were Chekhov and Eudora Welty.

We could say that this is simply a matter of our living in a fallen world, an example of what St. Paul meant when he said, "The good I would do, I do not do." But it is one thing to say that we can fail in our attempts to live decently, to be good; it is another to live with what seems to be a radical disconnection between the realm of the beautiful and any truth worth living for. Is there no insight in Bach or Rilke; or, if there is, does it have anything to do with the truths we must live by?

We need a larger frame, I think. We are still working with some notions that come down to us from the Enlightenment and from the Romantic movement. From the Enlightenment we get the idea that to understand something rationally is to understand it sufficiently. (This is the mentality that says that theology could be taught as well by an atheist as by a believer, to the extent that theology is a consistent intellectual endeavor.) The Romantics, who reacted to smug certainties of the Enlightenment, have given us the idea that to understand something completely we must understand it emotionally, from within. We have somehow wedded these contradictory ideas in our understanding of moral education. We can't understand the Nazi who weeps at Mozart in the evening and gasses people in the morning because we have been taught that exposure to high culture makes us better people.

The place in which the aesthetic and religious are most clearly wedded is the icon. Many icons are extraordinarily beautiful. Rublev's icon of the Holy Trinity is an example of the sort of art before which you are brought to stillness. But in an important sense, that isn't the point. Some Orthodox saints prayed before icons that were dreadful, artistically, and some horrible Orthodox live surrounded by lovely icons.

An experience cannot, in and of itself, educate us or form us; this is the Romantic fallacy. Nor can the application of reason or a set of standards educate us. (This could be called the rationalistic or canonical fallacy.) Both must be understood within a greater context.

A person who is formed by prayer, by liturgy, by ascetic struggle, will respond to the world differently from someone who is constantly distracted, who never worships, who responds to every desire by yielding to it. Most of us probably live somewhere between those two poles.

The question is not only one of responding to the world differently, but has to do also with our capacity for seeing the world. We bring the formed self—formed either by prayer or by distraction—to how we reason, to how we envision the world. An experience of overwhelming beauty might bring even the most evil person to a kind of stillness, but if the larger context is lacking, if no serious demand has ever been made on that person, it will remain merely an overwhelming aesthetic experience. We have allowed the Enlightenment and the Romantic strains in our culture to limit our understanding: we believe that things are known rationally or emotionally. We must consider the fact that the world can also be understood spiritually, and this dimension is not a variant of the subjective realm of emotion or the objective realm of reason, but has its own objectivity and subjectivity.

This brings us back to the idea of apatheia. Kallistos Ware points out that "the dispassioned person, so far from being apathetic, is the one whose heart burns with love for God, for other humans, for every living creature, for all that God has made (*The*

Orthodox Way, St. Vladimir's Seminary Press, 1981). He quotes St. Isaac the Syrian: "The heart of such a man grows tender, and he cannot endure to hear of or look upon any injury, even the smallest suffering, inflicted upon anything in creation. Therefore he never ceases to pray with tears even for the dumb animals, for the enemies of truth, and for all who do harm to it, asking that they may be guarded and receive God's mercy. And for the reptiles also he prays with great compassion, which rises up endlessly in his heart after the example of God."

The beauty which brings us to stillness, in Bach or in Rublev's icon of the Trinity, can be fully understood, can change us, only if someone has brought this wider living, the truer understanding, to his or her seeing. The idea of right understanding, truer observation, seems elitist in a time that doesn't feel comfortable with hierarchies of any sort, or the idea that there may be a privileged understanding—a kind of knowing more real than another. It is this more real knowing, a knowing different from and more important than reason or emotion, that Jesus pointed to when he said, "He who has ears, let him hear." But the hierarchy is necessary: without it we are left with the concentration camp guard and the great theologian Karl Barth, both lovers of Mozart, both equals in the only kinds of understanding our age allows.

Chapter 11

Love Incarnate

First, two poems—one from the beginning of (more or less) modern English, the other contemporary.

Western wind, when will thou blow,
    The small rain down can rain?
Christ, if my love were in my arms
    And I in my bed again!

This was written by the always prolific Anonymous, probably during the late fifteenth or early sixteenth century. The second poem:

Wide, wide in the rose's side
    Sleeps a child without sin,
And any man who loves in this world
    Stands here on guard over him.

This was written by the American poet Kenneth Patchen in 1957. What fascinates me about both poems is that although they are separated by four centuries, they are metrically similar; both are also about love (which, Yeats said, is the only thing other than death that adults can take seriously), and have an immediate power. One is about a specific and erotic longing, the other about something equally specific— a kind of universal paternal love—that is fierce and wonderful and reminds me of Blake, as much of Patchen's work does. The importance of these poems for me is not only literary but has to do with how we think of love—the particular love we have for the one we want to take into our arms, which has to do with the larger loves.

Although love in practice can be the most complicated thing in the world, it is not hard for us to understand at one level. Whether we talk about the love of husband for wife or parents for children, there is something helpless about love, something that takes us out of ourselves, whether we like it or not. Infatuation, often the beginning of erotic love, can be overwhelming and distressing, inconvenient. The love of a parent for a child is not a choice; it is a force that impinges itself on your life. Even abused children understand that at some level their parents should love them, and want to love the abusive parent. The bitterness that leads to further abuse, as in the case of the abused child who grows into an abusive parent, is a reaction to a profound betrayal, a betrayal of something primordial. There is here something close to an absolute: the person to whom evil has been done knows that the world should not be this way, that things are meant to be different, that real love never behaves like this…Love is in this sense like gravity, and where it should be and is not there is the sense of something against the grain, something unnatural.

I remember a lame defense of clerical celibacy that went something like this: the married man or woman loves one person, and the celibate is freed to love all persons equally. There are good arguments for celibacy (at least for monks and nuns, if not for parish priests), but this is not one of them. A person who has not loved a particular person is not capable of loving anyone, much less many people. That love may or may not be erotic, but it has to be for a particular person. Love doesn't exist "in general." "Western Wind" shows us a specific, erotic yearning; "Wide, Wide in the Rose's Side" shows us a child, and from the child we go to all love, to anyone who loves—but it begins with one bit of flesh, bone, beating heart.

In John's account of the Last Supper, Jesus tells his disciples, "As the Father has loved me, so I have loved you; abide in my love…This is my commandment, that you love one another as I have loved you" (John 15: 9,12). And Matthew 25 makes it clear that this love must take concrete form: whatever you do for "the least of these my brethren" is done for the Lord. The righteous and unrighteous alike ask, "When did we see you hungry, thirsty, a stranger, sick, in prison?" Any true act of compassion—whether done for consciously Christian reasons or not—is a work in which the love of God is incarnate. And it is on the basis of these acts of love that we will be judged, and, according to Matthew 25, this incarnate love is the only criterion for our judgement.

I once heard a report on National Public Radio that told of a remarkable example of compassion. The reporter, Diana Nyad, was part of a cycling tour of Vietnam; the tour included a number of American veterans who had been wounded during the war in Vietnam. During a meeting with Vietnamese schoolchildren, one of the tour members was asked about his worst memory of the war. Most of the listeners expected him to speak of his own injuries. Instead, he told of entering a village with orders to kill the first person he met who could spread the alarm about the advancing American troops. The first person he encountered was a boy of about eight, who was armed, and as the veteran tried to tell the story, he wept: he had killed the child. One of the children, seeing his tears, began to weep too, and went over to him and put her arms around him. I have no idea if she was a Buddhist, a Christian, or a believer of any sort, but the compassionate love of God was certainly present in that moment, and in the specific gesture of taking the weeping man in her arms.

Chapter 12

The Radiant Scandal

George Steiner—one of our greatest modern critics and one of the few who takes theology seriously—compares the writings surrounding Socrates and Jesus in a chapter of *No Passion Spent* (Yale University Press, 1996). At the end of "Two Cocks," a powerful and challenging essay in which he firmly rejects any fundamentalist or literalist approach to Scripture, Steiner writes: "Reason as I can, there are passages in the Old and New Testaments which I am unable to accord with any sensible image, however exalted, of normal authorship, of conception and composition as we seek to grasp them in even the greatest of thinkers and poets. Mundane imaginings are almost wholly rebuked by, for example, the thought of Shakespeare coming home for lunch and reporting on whether the writing of acts 3 and 4 of King Lear 'had gone well.' Almost. Considered reflection does allow such a vignette its place at the far edges of the ordinary. As I have remarked earlier, I am at a loss when, by analogy or similitude, I try to graft this picture onto the author of the speeches out of the whirlwind in Job. When I would apply it to certain sequences in the Psalms or Ecclesiastes. When I would explain to myself the genesis of such pericopes in the Gospels as Jesus' 'Before Abraham was, I am' or of very nearly the entirety of chapters 13-17 in John. In such biblical instances, the concept of a wholly rational hermeneutic escapes me. I find myself backed up against the harsh radiance of 'the scandalous.'"

This points to something beyond either fundamentalism or its denial, to a claim that is put upon us at a level so close to the bone that it approaches the demand Jesus made of his followers: "Who do you say that I am?" And Steiner's choices are good ones. Anyone who can read God's answer to Job without the short hairs rising on the back of his neck is braindead.

This passage brought me back to a recurrent thought: belief is always based on a response to something less than clear and compelling evidence, and the old notion that one could be led logically, by argument, to faith is not only wrong but possibly a form of blasphemy. If faith could be proven, you would have the proof, and lose God. What you do get, and all you get, is a clue. It orients you. You have a choice: go with this, or lose track. It is the direction you are moving in that is the sign of faith. In The Mystery of Jesus (a section of *Pensees*), Pascal has the Lord say, "If you are seeking me, you have found me." The clue can be faint, the way you look at some stars in deep darkness by not seeing them directly, but by looking at the dark next to them. You have the hope that it is God leading, and not illusion or self-deception, that gets you to this place. Trust in God is nothing like a claim on him, or ownership, or a sense of absolute certainty.

And yet there is something compelling here. The faint star really is there, there is an authority about some passages in Scripture, some people you have met, some stories you have heard, that doesn't exist anywhere else. This is something you sense viscerally, and you hope it is true, and try to stake your life on not being deceived in this. It isn't proof. But there are moments when something cuts through our reading to our hearts.

The story of Zacchaeus, his enthusiasm, and the sweet detail of a short man climbing a sycamore tree to see Jesus; the four short verses in the parable of the Pharisee and the tax collector; the parable of the prodigal son and his merciful father—if this sort of storytelling is not in some profound way divine inspiration, something in us needs it to be; if this is not true, why worry about truth at all? The power and beauty of these passages make us understand what

Dostoevski meant when he said that if he had to choose between the truth and Christ, he would choose Christ. (Simone Weil, citing this, pointed out that Christ—the way, the truth, and the life—would rather Dostoevski choose the truth.)

Dostoevski was a romantic who could also say, "Beauty will save the world." At nineteen you breathe, "Yes!" But then you remember the concentration camp guard weeping at Mozart. Sorry, beauty isn't enough. Dostoevski also wrote, in commenting on his composition of the chapters "Rebellion" and "The Grand Inquisitor" in *The Brothers Karamazov*, that his "hosannah of belief" was "forged in the crucible of great doubt." That may be closer to the experience of many of us.

The passages that Steiner cites do something beautiful and powerful; so does much great art. The parables of Jesus are succinct, charged examples of perfect storytelling. But more: they bring you to a stop. Without offering anything like proof, they speak with such authority that—beyond proof or disproof, certainty or doubt—they make me think that if this is not the truth about God and God's relationship to us, nothing is; and that can be enough to bring someone to the edge of faith, "the assurance of things hoped for, the conviction of things not seen" (Hebrews 11:1). I know how passages from John's gospel worked on one person.

During the time when communism in Albania had crushed religion, or tried to, a young man of Muslim background was given a copy of a book in French by someone who knew his love of French literature. The person who gave him the book was not aware that it was a French translation of the Gospel according to St. John. The young man read it and knew that he had to become a Christian. As others stood guard looking out for the secret police, he was baptized in the basement of a priest who, at great risk to his life, had continued to serve the church. The young man left Albania, became a monk, and later returned to serve the church, after the fall of communism. He is now Metropolitan John, the bishop of Korce.

The fact that he is now a bishop where once he might have been murdered for his faith is wonderful, but what moves me most is the thought of his encounter with the word of God in John, and the knowledge that he must become a Christian. That moment is full of the radiance not only of "the scandalous," but a reminder that the power at work among us is the power that raised Jesus Christ from the dead.

Chapter 13

The Depth of the Story

A few years ago Joyce Carol Oates wrote an op-ed page piece in the *New York Times*, and said something which reflects the thinking of many of our contemporaries: "The truth of one era becomes, as if by an artist's slight of hand, the mythology of subsequent eras. What was sacred becomes secular. Our impassioned ancestors must have intended books like the Hebrew Bible and the New Testament to be historical documents, bearing the literal truth, not the metaphorical truth they embody today."

I am not sure that this is true—or at least it is not nearly so simple. For example, when the church compiled the New Testament it knowingly included some contradictory accounts. (The church determined which books would be considered part of the canon largely in reaction to Marcion, who wanted to exclude all of the Old Testament, and much of what became the New Testament.) The genealogies of Jesus offered by Matthew and Luke, for example, are different; the chronologies of John and the synoptic Gospels differ, and these and other differences—how many angels appeared at the tomb after the resurrection, and what did they say?—were noted early on.

The compilers of the Hebrew Bible also had no problem with contradiction: the two creation accounts in Genesis differ, to take only one example. And you can read the story of Jonah as a wonderful (and funny) fable, and the account of the three young men in the fiery furnace, in Daniel, was plainly composed for lively recitation. And what could history have to do with the Song of Songs?

My problem is not with the idea that our ancestors may have had a different approach to these things than we do, nor do I deny that they may have thought Jonah was really swallowed by a huge fish. My problem is with a too simple distinction between "literal truth" and "metaphorical truth." Our modern idea of history is relatively recent, and limited: just the facts, please. A radical cleavage is made between the idea of the objective and the subjective. One of the points Oates wanted to make in her essay is that it isn't that simple, and she is right. But was the Bible ever intended primarily as "history" or "literal truth," and can this be separated from "metaphorical truth"?

When Jesus spoke of the prodigal son and his merciful father, or of the Pharisee and the tax collector, he was telling stories. Not even a fundamentalist would deny that there was no historical prodigal son, but Jesus says, "There was a man who had two sons..." Was he lying about history? What if Jesus himself never said it, but this was Luke's way of getting across part of Jesus' teaching? The point here is not history. What we have to see is that the prodigal son and his merciful father are, in a way we must learn to understand or miss the point of Christianity, more real than Warren Harding or the Teapot Dome scandal. There are truths that are historical, and more than historical; and there are truths that can be expressed metaphorically, but they are more than metaphors. Facts and history do not exhaust reality, and metaphors either point to something true or they do not. An elegant and aesthetically pleasing metaphor may be dead wrong, and a homely one right on target.

This has to do, finally, with recovering a way of understanding that we have lost. This could be the most important meaning of tradition, which means "what is handed on." Origen knew, in the third century, that Paul did not write the Letter to the Hebrews which had been attributed to him, but he knew that what mattered was the text, not the author. Matthew has Jesus speak from a mountain (to be like Moses); Luke puts his different version of the same set of teachings on a plain. What matters what is said: Love your enemies, forgive one another as God has forgiven you. The rest really is distraction because the more you hang around these words, the more you can see the consistency and understand that the different nuances also instruct, like midrash, the form of story-telling that illuminates a text. In one commentary on Exodus which employs midrash, the angels who rejoice in the drowning of Pharoah's troops are silenced by the Lord, who say, "How dare you rejoice, when my creatures, the Egyptians, are dying?" The point is not to add new history to old history, or to argue that the account in Exodus is deficient as history. We are talking about something more than history here.

This approach to what we read and what we hear has traditionally been part of biblical interpretation. Next to this richness, too simple a distinction between literal and metaphorical truth seems pretty thin. And because of the limitations of our own mindset, we can run the danger of saying that if it isn't a "fact" or historical, it must be "merely" metaphorical. What we have to understand is that something as real as the Resurrection—which I believe truly happened—cannot be confined by history, which is only our account of things. There is a reality beyond our accounting, and we need a language richer than the language of history to get at it.

Chapter 14

Suffering and God's Compassion

Our society is probably the first in which we agree to keep what matters most to us out of our common discourse, because it could divide us. Combine the secular basis of liberal democracy with capitalism, and you get a society in which civic order and the need for distraction become the most valued commodities.

In traditional societies one religion usually reigned. Members of minority communities were tolerated at best or slaughtered. The separation of church and state has at least freed religion from its alliance with coercive power, and where no particular advantage can be gained from religious affiliation, a faith may be chosen clearly and honestly.

But the price paid for this is that we see religion placed in the realm of the subjective, a matter of taste. The differences involved in religion divide us, and what unites us is considered much more important—but what is that, in our secular society? The marketplace, not only of ideas but of commodities—or rather, ideas become commodities, and the ones we like best are the ones we accept as true. The successful sale of a commodity demands that the thing we are being sold—cars, whiskey, brand-name clothes, bottled water, religion—can satisfy us and make us whole now, and we will not be happy (being happy is all-important) unless we buy, or buy into, what is being offered for sale.

Our culture tells us this at every turn, and the con-sequences are tragic. The irony is that the tragedy lies in the avoidance of the tragic. If one thing is central to the understanding of all great religious traditions, it is that there is something divided and strange, some-thing broken and unhappy, about the world we find ourselves in, and if this can be corrected at all (not at all a sure thing) it will be at a cost; it will involve a struggle, even death.

Traditional societies could put the stories that tell this truth at the center, even while they avoided its implications at every opportunity. Our society turns the ad volume up and asks us to look at anything but the one unavoidable fact: there is, for all of us, a 100-per-cent mortality rate, and all the fitness centers and careful diets and state-of-the-art medications will not help us out of that hole.

The first of the Buddha's "four noble truths" is that existence is suffering. At the center of the gospel message we find the crucifixion. To redeem us, Jesus had to come to where we are, and the cross is where humanity is. The Resurrection, which gives us hope, has happened only to him, and our faith is that he will "come again in glory" to judge us mercifully. But the truth of our world, this side of our own resurrection, is Golgotha, the place of the cross. We have crucified the Lord of glory, we continue to torment and kill one another, and we are tormented ourselves. And we have been given the power to forgive and be forgiven, to love, even to die for the sake of another. But none of this has to do with the satisfaction of our immediate desire, and our culture—based as it is on commerce— is established on the creation of new desires and the illusion that they can be satisfied.

So many people find it hard to accept the absolute unavoidability of suffering. You hear it constantly: "Why did she have to suffer? She was such a good person..." As if goodness were a hedge against suffering. The suffering of the just is an ancient mystery, at least as old as Job. It shows us a truer picture of the world than our temporary comfort. Just or unjust, we will all be crucified. God's mercy falls on the just and unjust alike, and so does suffering.

The greater mystery is that at the base of suffering there is something profoundly moving and even hopeful in a way which is hard to explain, and perhaps it can only be experienced. A young woman asked me to visit her fiance, a young man who has been in a coma for sixteen months. I have been to see him with her a couple of times, to anoint him and pray with her and with his family. She goes to see him for hours every day after work, in a hospital where there are many like him, a bleak place where there are few visitors. She talks with him, reads to him, turns him in his bed to make sure he doesn't get bedsores. She hopes for a miracle, but her love doesn't depend on one. She will wait, and nothing may happen. What is constant is her patient love, a love which hopes, but without demanding results, a love which endures without any clear expectation. This is already a miracle. There is something prophetic about this kind of love—it shows us something we need to know about God's love for us, for all the suffering world.

Another example: a little boy in my parish, about two years old, who has had a bone marrow transplant which will, his family hopes, cure a rare childhood form of leukemia. I try to see him and his family once a week, and have to scrub up and put on a sterile gown and gloves to enter the hospital unit he is staying in. His parents and grandparents take shifts, to make sure someone is with him constantly.

It is heartbreaking, but at the same time there is something beautiful about it. His family is so loving and attentive, the medical staff so compassionate, that you know something holy is happening here, as well as something deeply sad. At times like this I am reminded of my first visceral experience of fatherhood. My daughter was born prematurely and almost died. I remember looking at her through two panes of glass and knowing that I would die to keep her alive.

That experience helped me realize what it means when we call God "father": the love shown in Christ, who referred to God as "father" constantly, is a powerful example of that fierce love. It is important to emphasize the ferocity because centuries of philosophy and theology have accustomed us to thinking of God as an impassive source of being, one who is beyond suffering, detached from the experience of our agony. But this is not biblical so much as it is a development of Greek philosophy. Pascal is more biblical when he says that Christ suffers until the end of time. Jesus tells Philip at the Last Supper discourse in John's gospel, "He who sees me has seen the Father." This is said by someone who is about to die for us.

When we refer to God as compassionate, we often think of the word as meaning something like "merciful" or "loving," and of course it does mean those things, but the word itself means, at root, "suffering with." You are only one with another person when you are capable of suffering with her, when your life has become so close that her suffering is your suffering. Love is not serious without compassion.

This is what makes baptism scary. We are baptized into Christ's death and the hope of his Resurrection. He has joined our lives with his; but we have joined his life with ours, which means we agree to live as he did. And that agreement calls us to a willingness even to die, to live like people who have died and have nothing to fear from death.

Most of us are very far from this. At moments when we are forced into suffering with another, as the sick child's parents and grandparents are, we begin to know something more about God's love for us. It is a painful knowledge. It leads some people to question God's goodness: we would rather have a God who fixes things than one who suffers with us. Even if we believe that at the end the suffering will be over, that resurrection and glory are the true end of the tale, we take little comfort from this as we look into the face of a suffering child, or see someone fading into Alzheimer's disease. In fact, seeking comfort seems almost indecent in these contexts; it is as if we are avoiding the horror of suffering, the full tragedy.

Orthodox Christianity teaches us that God does not will human suffering; it is the result of sin. This can hardly be demonstrated in any philosophically satisfying way. But we can see that compassion and suffering are connected, and so are compassion and forgiveness. To forgive without compassion is not really forgiveness, just as a truce is not really peace.

Real forgiveness understands the offender with love and compassion, not excusing the offense, but understanding the pain, the woundedness, from which almost every offense proceeds. If Christ is the one through whom we are forgiven and reconciled, if we are baptized into his death and the hope of resurrection, we can learn what this means only by entering into a life which risks being wounded. This is what compassion involves.

And unsatisfying as this may be—it doesn't, after all, fix every situation, and the people towards whom we are compassionate will die, and some of them will continue to hate us—it is the only way we can begin to approach the mystery of Christ's life among us and within us.

Christianity is not a philosophy. An Albanian monk once spoke to some of our parishioners, immigrants from Albania, where the persecution of their relatives under the repressive communist regime made many of them bitter. One man had a particularly hard time accepting the idea that we must forgive our enemies. The monk—now Metropolitan John of Korce—told him that you cannot reason your way to the forgiveness of enemies; it has been commanded by someone who forgives us, but can forgive us only if we forgive others. We become capable of being forgiven only when we are truly capable of forgiving.

If there ever was anything to the idea that God is beyond suffering, it may be because God lives where it has all been accomplished, and knows how the story ends.

There is little here that is abstract. It is all about relationships between persons; this is what the doctrine of the Trinity means, among other things. No self, not even God's self, exists in isolation. God's unknowable self has been revealed in flesh and blood and bone. During my seminary years, one of my best teachers tried to cut through the ways in which seminarians—and many other Christians—tend to theologize: "You strike me," he said, "and I refuse to strike you back, and this is how we discuss the Trinity."

Chapter 15

When the Church Gets in the Way

You hear people say that it is difficult to be a believer in our society. Though there are many ways in which this is true, we should reexamine the idea. America is, after all, more religious than most nations. It is certainly easier to be a Christian now than it was under the Emperor Decius. That very ease may be part of the problem, but it is only a part of it. Unease—a profound unease—is also involved.

What does it mean to assert a belief in God—or, for that matter, belief in the possibility of encountering any transforming truth—in our kind of society? To a serious believer it must mean more than simply, "this is to my taste."

Belief competes with many alternatives. One of them is indifference, a sense that is not really agnosticism but a kind of "so what?" Principled agnosticism can be intellectually admirable, even sympathetic; indifference is not. It is the result of a culture that has placed distraction and gratification so firmly at the center that they completely dominate the lives of millions, including many people who remain culturally attached to churches, synagogues, mosques, or temples, people who often think of themselves as in some sense religious. These buildings and the holidays associated with them are not central to their lives in any important way. They are more like "our song"; their hold is at best sentimental.

One piece of this problem is not uniquely contemporary. Other cultures have paid lip service to religion, while paying their real attention to money, power, and pleasure. We have placed wealth and reverence for wealth not only at the center—most other cultures have done that—but a particular kind of wealth, a particular kind of fame and celebrity. Mother Teresa, Princess Diana, Richard Gere, and the Pope are all similarly candidates for the cover of *People*, and therefore equally important. When religious leaders regard it as a coup to be endorsed by celebrities, or to receive an award from Congress, or to be photographed with presidents and senators, they become part of the problem. When Dorothy Day was told that some people considered her a saint, she famously said, "I won't be dismissed that easily." People who allow themselves to be seduced by the aura of celebrity make themselves, and the religion they claim to represent, dismissible.

There is another chilling side to indifference. For many people, it appears to be as easy to drop a religion as it is to lose an umbrella. This is where the unease enters. How can something which claims to be about so much that matters—our reason for being in the world, the story of one who died for us—be so easily laid aside?

I have known people raised in constricting Catholic, Jewish, Evangelical, and Eastern Orthodox environments, who rejected their religious traditions in anger or disappointment. While disagreeing, I can understand the emotional and familial dynamics involved in their drifting away. I am more troubled by friends whose excuses seem too easy. These don't involve serious doubts or difficult family backgrounds. Liturgical boredom is enough, or the feeling that church takes too much time. This seems too little a reason to sever a connection that should (given what we say it is about) be more vital, more urgent.

I have heard that in Ireland, after clergy and hierarchy were involved in sexual scandals, there was a notable falling away from religious practice, not only among the young, but especially in those over fifty. I have seen a small Orthodox parish reduced to nearly nothing by a sexual scandal involving the priest. Many Roman Catholics have found themselves unable to attend Mass because of scandals involving pedophile priests. I can understand this reaction, up to a point. It is, after all, the clergy and the hierarchy who insist on the continuing validity of traditional norms which restrict sexual activity to married men and women. They are the transmitters not only of this teaching, but of all the sacraments. Sexual fidelity and honoring one's word (whether this involves a vow of marriage or a commitment to celibacy) go to the heart of who we are. It is easy to see how someone faced with hypocrisy and deception in this area (or to be more charitable than I am inclined to be, with weakness where honor and honesty are concerned) would simply abandon the whole thing.

And still, much as I can sympathize with the disgust of the leave-takers, I think they are wrong; even more wrong are those who can spend a life around the story of Jesus and remain unmoved enough to leave the church because of their boredom. There is a tone-deafness here which is largely the fault of the church, but this does not absolve each of us from the duty to try to hear, through all the hypocrisy and boredom, the words of Jesus, or to try to see what it means that someone loves us enough to die for us. If the behavior of bishops and priests seems to stand in the way—if at times the church itself seems to—we have to remember that even at the Last Supper, even in the act of blessing the bread and wine, Jesus tells us, "This cup is the new covenant in my blood, which is poured out for you. But the hand of him who is going to betray me is with mine on the table" (Luke 22: 20-21). Betrayal and duplicity were there from the start.

Those who feel betrayed by their experience of the church are not wrong in their feeling, but they have a duty to the rest of the body to which they have been joined in baptism. When the Orthodox Church in Russia was, institutionally, a weak and subservient department of the state, there were saints whose lives illuminated the lives of those around them. The church in Francis of Assisi's day was a mess, and saints have lived under thoroughly corrupt popes. It is the duty of baptized people to be Christians, too often despite the people who are supposed to lead them.

The greatest danger of our culture, in making a religious commitment something like a consumer choice, is that we will not see that this commitment is finally a matter of life and death, for us and for a much larger community, one to which we have an obligation. Our culture allows us to take nothing seriously except what we perceive to be our needs and desires. Unless these have been informed by a relationship with the living God, they will mislead us.

If the church itself does not offer a way towards that relationship, or in practice can even stand in its way, it is still our obligation to dig more deeply into the tradition, to try to hear the voice of Jesus—even when we feel entombed, like Lazarus. The church is necessary because we cannot break the bread and drink the wine alone. Jesus asks in Luke 18:8, "When the Son of Man comes, will he find faith on earth?" Perhaps our hope lies in the restoration of this eschatological understanding that the Lord is coming, and our deepest vocation is to be aware of that, despite everything in the culture, even in the church, that may seem to stand in his way.

Chapter 16

Religion, Superstition, and Religious Agnosticism

The rhetoric of some atheists and agnostics makes it appear that there is a fine line—if indeed there is any line at all—between religion and superstition. Religious people should be careful not to be too defensive about this because it is often true. There is, in fact, a form of religion which is akin to carrying a lucky rabbit's foot or knocking on wood, and it is more pervasive in our churches than we want to acknowledge. You encounter it when people find themselves in some personal crisis and ask, "How could this happen to me? I have always gone to church, tried to live a Christian life…" as if we will be rewarded for such things. Life may be an automatic death sentence, but some of us are apparently supposed to get time off for good behavior.

You have to sympathize with people who ask this sort of question, because they are in real pain, and are genuinely baffled: the God who was supposed to make good things happen if you are nice isn't coming through. This has to be dealt with pastorally and sensitively, but it does confirm the agnostic view of religion as a crutch, a shield against the harsh realities of the world, a comforting illusion. The atheist or agnostic looks at people crowding their way towards the shrine at Guadalupe or venerating a wonderworking icon, and can't help contrasting this with a starving child, whose parents are no doubt praying for her survival as fervently as anyone ever prayed. It is easy to find something obscene in the idea that God arbitrarily rewards some while others suffer horribly. There is no comfort, or even any convincing answer, in the idea that God's ways are not our ways. That's true, in spades, but it is hardly an argument.

Part of the problem with any theodicy is the notion that God is powerful in the sense that we ordinarily give that word. Theodicy has been reduced to the formula, "If God is good he is not God; if God is God he is not good." God being God here means being the one who makes everything happen the way it happens, God as the set designer, playwright, director, puppet master. There is something of this picture of God in the Bible itself, but there are other strands there that also need attention. Christians too often see the revelation of Jesus Christ as something added to this picture of God as all powerful (in the directorial

120

sense mentioned above) and not as something that radically inverts and challenges it. Such attempts as process theology or Tielhard de Chardin's evolving cosmos continue the attempt to save God's virtue, while making him less than completely powerful: the idea is that the picture is not yet complete.

This sort of thinking should be resisted. The power revealed in Christ upsets all ideas of power as control, even evolving control. What I want to suggest involves no more than a couple of hints, and maybe that's as good as we'll ever get. God's presence is made manifest not only in acts of compassion and self-sacrifice; it is present to us only when we place ourselves there, where God has been in the flesh. We can begin to discern God's will and God's presence only when we are, to some extent, like God; and any attempt to go beyond that—in explanation, in thought—is vain. Jesus tells us we will not be forgiven if we do not forgive, that we are to love even our enemies, that whatever we do for the least human being is done for God. God's strength is revealed in absolute powerlessness—from our point of view—in the death of Christ on the cross. He has collapsed the distance between divine immutability and human suffering, and the initiative is all from his side, but we are invited to participate, and told that the consequences will be serious if we do not.

Beyond this, I think we should be willing to know nothing. We have to answer, "How could a good God permit such suffering?" with a non-answer: "I have no idea, except that he stood where the suffering are, and suffered with them." When Jesus says "He who has seen me has seen the Father," he tells us both that this is the kind of God we have, and also that this is all we can know of him. The rest is hidden, and is meant to be. The hiddenness calls us to trust, to a living, and therefore risky, relationship. As in any serious relationship—like marriage or parenthood—we live with the faith and hope that things will turn out wonderfully, but, this side of the end, we can't be absolutely sure. It isn't our place, at this point, to know the results or the end of the story, other than to try to trust the one who tells us.

It is fascinating that Jesus himself is, in a sense, hidden following the Resurrection. Mary Magdalene mistakes him for the gardener; the disciples on the shore do not recognize him until they fill their nets; the disciples on the road to Emmaus do not know the one with whom they have been talking until they recognize him in the breaking of the bread. And most significantly, at the end of Matthew's gospel, he has gathered them on the mountain: "And when they saw him they worshiped him; but some doubted." Some doubted: it is clear that something was not entirely clear. It was not obvious that this was the risen Lord

Jesus, the same one who had been crucified. This hiddenness may be the way in which he initiates us into the reality that whatever we do for the least human being, we do for him. And our doubtfulness—our ordinary half-hoping, half-doubting faith—is not an excuse to avoid the mission. To all of those gathered on the mountain, including those who doubted, he says, "Go therefore and make disciples of all nations..." It is significant that at this appearance Matthew's account says that, seeing him, "some doubted." But the charge was given to all.

The criticism of atheists and agnostics, mentioned above, is not about to vanish—not even if Christians begin to act as if they took the gospel seriously. The belief that life has any inherent meaning is itself an act of faith and can't be demonstrated. Chesterton says, somewhere, that the problem many agnostics and atheists have with Christianity is not that it is not good news, but rather that the news is too good to be true. There is something bracing about the idea of trying to live an honest and moral life in a universe where honesty and morality are fragile but essential human traits, played out against an indifferent background. Even the noblest Christian looks, to someone who sincerely thinks this way, a bit like a child with an imaginary friend. Our hope for people who think this way is that in the end they will be wonderfully surprised.

"For you have died, and your life is hid with Christ in God. When Christ who is our life appears, then you also will appear with him in glory" (Colossians 3:3). The hiddenness that is an essential aspect of the risen Christ applies also to us, and to our own lives this side of death. We are largely hidden from ourselves. We do not know how we might react if put to the test, though we may imagine we would be noble; and we pray, appropriately, in words the Lord gave us, "Lead us not into temptation," which is better translated, "Do not put us to the test…" Those who have been forced to bear witness, and have come through, give us hope. They reflect the reality we see in Christ crucified and in the hope of his Resurrection. The only contact that we will have with this reality, on this side of our resurrection, is found in the face of anyone suffering—anyone, finally, born and on the way to death. The rest is as hidden from us as it is from any agnostic, which should make us understand our brotherhood.

Other books by John Garvey:

Modern Spirituality: An Anthology

Orthodoxy for the Non-Orthodox:
A Brief Introduction to Orthodox Christianity

The Prematurely Saved
and Other Varieties of the Religious Experience